CHANGE YOUR LIFE WITH
FENG SHUI

PAK-TIN LI AND HELEN YEAP

quantum

LONDON • NEW YORK • TORONTO • SYDNEY

quantum

The Publishing House, Bennetts Close,
Cippenham, Berkshire SL1 5AP, England.

ISBN 0-572-02301-4

Printed in Great Britain by
St Edmundsbury Press,
Bury St Edmunds, Suffolk

Contents

What is Feng Shui?

The Chinese art of Feng Shui is both ancient and highly complex. Put simply, Feng Shui is the art of placing buildings and objects in relation to energy, to accentuate the positive elements and minimise those which are negative.

Feng Shui literally means 'wind and water', and these are the two most significant features in the art. Ch'i energy moves on the winds, while water nourishes the soil. Mountains offer a vantage point and shelter from harsh winds, and these also play an important role.

Feng Shui links and interacts with the movement of Ch'i energy; with the balancing feminine and masculine characteristics of Yin and Yang; with the five Chinese elements of earth, metal, water, wood and fire; and with Chinese astrology.

Underlying the principles of Feng Shui is the idea of Ch'i, the animating life-force that exists everywhere and permeates both ourselves and our homes and physical surroundings. Ch'i energy is positive when allowed to flow freely, negative when left to stagnate in nooks and crannies, and harmful when channelled too quickly along straight paths.

The purpose of Feng Shui, the art of placement, is to enable you to organise your home so that the Ch'i energy has free movement and is not allowed either to stagnate or to accelerate too quickly. To achieve this, you use precise placement of furniture and belongings or symbolic objects to remove barriers to the free flow of Ch'i. The result of this is that you can tap into the beneficial, positive Ch'i energy to the maximum, and disperse, disrupt or remove negative energy. This understanding and recognition of the positive features that enhance the free flow of energy will have a direct impact on your well-being and financial prosperity.

Allied to this is the concept of complementary forces of Yin and Yang – light and dark – the polar opposites of all existence. Yin is the feminine element and Yang is the masculine element. When they blend together to create balance, harmony reigns.

With the motion of the earth, astral and magnetic influences vary, affecting different people to different degrees. Applied to people, Feng Shui is about fine-tuning our physical surroundings to harmonise with our inner life-force, Ch'i, based on the premise that an imbalance of energies displaces good luck and brings about internal disorders.

These same concepts can be applied to buildings, whether homes, factories or offices, and to the furniture and decoration we place in those buildings.

Homes are bought or chosen every day and are the base from which we live our lives. So it is vital that the largest single investment most individuals make harmonises with the living land and is positioned so that it is poised to ride the winds of prosperity, health and longevity. When we choose a house, we can consider these factors before we select it. If we have already selected our home, we can assess its features and make changes – simple changes of the placement of furniture or symbolic gestures such as using blinds or curtains – which will place the house and its contents and occupants in a position of harmony with the energies of the life-force, and harness the positive elements that will change our lives.

The purpose of having a house Feng Shui-ed is to make that assessment; to discover the movement of energies through the house and – relating that to the specific birth signs and elements of the occupants – choose the best use of rooms, the optimum placement of furniture, even the decor and colour schemes. For example, you can select the best room to use as an office, and the particular placement of a desk that will encourage success. You can take steps to ensure that the crucial main door is providing an entry point for the positive flow of energy into the house. Using Feng Shui will also help you to confine any negative energies in the home, preventing them from circulating about the rest of the house.

These are some of the many balancing and compensating uses of Feng Shui, namely the symbolic unlocking of energy meridians through the positioning, removing and counterbalancing of obstacles.

There are many manifestations of just how dark and dismal life on the wrong side of Feng Shui can become. Relationships can fail, careers can stagnate and financial opportunities can be lost, to give you a few examples. Fortunately, there are solutions to all eventualities, straightforward actions that you can take to accentuate the positive and eliminate the negative. Of course, the much-revered Feng Shui expert can make the most precise calculations that strike the perfect compromise based on a person's date and time of birth and their corresponding energy meridian. This book cannot emulate that level of knowledge and expertise. It does, however, seek to give you an introduction to the art of Feng Shui, and to show you how you can make alterations to your home so that you can change your life for the better.

Because so many of the elements of Feng Shui are interactive, and this book aims to give a simple explanation of an ancient and complex topic, you will find it helpful to read through the chapters first to absorb all the facets of the subject before you try to look specifically at your own home. You will see that in order to illustrate the various aspects of the subject, the book features specific situations, the majority with illustrations, and explains the effects of their positive and negative influences. Following this are suggestions for altering the situation where necessary so that you can allow free flow of the positive energies. So you can check whether a situation applies to you, note its positive and negative elements, and find the appropriate solution.

Chapter 1

The Elements

Feng Shui concerns itself with people and their interaction with the earth, sun, sky, moon and stars. Everything – including people – is classified into one of the five elements: wood, fire, earth, metal and water. And each of the five elements has particular characteristics. These can each be energising or debilitating, according to how they interact with each other.

Personal elements

For everyone there is one particular personal element which will be as important to them as their Western Zodiac sign. In the Chinese system, it will have fundamental bearing on their astrological influences. In Chinese astrology, there are 12 animal signs which are assigned to each year in a pattern of rotation: rat, ox, tiger, rabbit, dragon, snake, horse, goat, monkey, rooster, dog, pig. Each year is also assigned one of the five elements.

The Chinese astrological year runs from around the 4th or 5th of February (the date varies each year), and the following table shows you the animal sign to which your year of birth belongs. For example, 1914 is the year of the tiger, 1915 is the year of the rabbit. The element relating to your personality and fortune would be worked out according to the date, time, month and year of your birth.

The characteristics of the elements

These are the elemental characteristics you may already be familiar with from Chinese astrology, and they can often be better understood by their symbolic nature. Thinking about the physical qualities of the elements gives a good indication of their psychological attributes and energy qualities.

Wood people have a strong personality. However, they can be easily influenced. They are helpful towards others, but tend to be fearful that others will try to control them or order them about.

Fire people are generous in friendship and always ready to help, but they tend to be unable to look after themselves.

Earth people are kind-hearted and always keep their word. On the other hand, they dislike advice and can be liable to change their minds.

Metal people spend money like water. By nature, they are generous, brave and helpful. Don't expect them to form long-term perspectives, or to take kindly to 'losing face'.

Water people are never petty. They are clever people and plan well ahead; however, they tend to be faint-hearted.

Personality characteristics relating to the elements

According to your animal sign, your personality will show specific characteristics. These will be further modified by the element relating to the year of your birth. In addition to this, you will exhibit other characteristics – both physically and in your personality – which relate to one particular element. If you visit a Chinese herbalist or acupuncturist they will probably diagnose your 'personality' element from these individual factors.

The elements and Feng Shui

This relationship with the personal element is important for understanding your personality and fortune. The way Feng Shui uses elements is different and should not be confused. The Feng Shui element relates to your year of birth and indicates which years are going to be the best years for you. The Feng Shui elements relating to the years are detailed in the following table.

For example, if you were born in 1958, your astrological sign is a dog and your Feng Shui element is earth. All the elements relate to each other in different ways, as you will see from the following section. For the man born in 1958, the compatible years are those assigned to earth and fire, and therefore earth and fire years will see him doing well. Decisions on investments and rapid progress should be made in those years. Wood years are those in which to take vacations.

The compatibility cycle

The elements in Feng Shui represent specific energies which relate closely to their natural characteristics. In the same way that different physical elements interact with each other either positively or negatively, you can see from the following chart how Feng Shui balances these elemental energies as compatible or incompatible.

In Feng Shui the compatibility cycle is based on a free-flowing circular movement, linking the elements in a positive combination of energies. Explaining the compatibility of energies by analogy is a good way of understanding how it works.

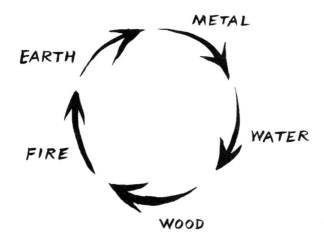

Wood feeds fire.

Fire, in the sense of volcanic activity, creates earth.

Earth is the cradle of ore and the creator of metal.

Metal in its molten form is solidified and finds its strength in water.

Water feeds the roots of trees and is at the heart of wood.

The incompatibility cycle

In the same way, analogous descriptions can help us to understand the negative interactions of energies.

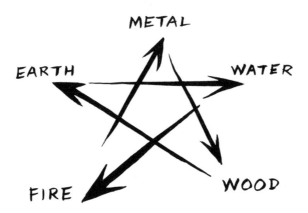

Wood, through its roots, drives stakes into the earth.

Earth smothers and consumes water.

Water extinguishes fire.

Fire corrodes metal.

Metal cuts wood.

Your Chinese animal signs and Feng Shui elements

The Chinese astrological year runs from about 4th or 5th of February in the ordinary calendar. If you were born in January, look up the previous year in this table.

Year	Chinese astrological sign	Feng Shui element
1914	Tiger	Wood
1915	Rabbit	Wood
1916	Dragon	Earth
1917	Snake	Fire
1918	Horse	Fire
1919	Goat	Earth
1920	Monkey	Metal
1921	Rooster	Metal
1922	Dog	Earth
1923	Pig	Water
1924	Rat	Water
1925	Ox	Earth
1926	Tiger	Wood
1927	Rabbit	Wood
1928	Dragon	Earth
1929	Snake	Fire
1930	Horse	Fire
1931	Goat	Earth
1932	Monkey	Metal
1933	Rooster	Metal
1934	Dog	Earth
1935	Pig	Water
1936	Rat	Water
1937	Ox	Earth
1938	Tiger	Wood

Year	Chinese astrological sign	Feng Shui element
1939	Rabbit	Wood
1940	Dragon	Earth
1941	Snake	Fire
1942	Horse	Fire
1943	Goat	Earth
1944	Monkey	Metal
1945	Rooster	Metal
1946	Dog	Earth
1947	Pig	Water
1948	Rat	Water
1949	Ox	Earth
1950	Tiger	Wood
1951	Rabbit	Wood
1952	Dragon	Earth
1953	Snake	Fire
1954	Horse	Fire
1955	Goat	Earth
1956	Monkey	Metal
1957	Rooster	Metal
1958	Dog	Earth
1959	Pig	Water
1960	Rat	Water
1961	Ox	Earth
1962	Tiger	Wood
1963	Rabbit	Wood
1964	Dragon	Earth
1965	Snake	Fire
1966	Horse	Fire
1967	Goat	Earth
1968	Monkey	Metal
1969	Rooster	Metal

Year	Chinese astrological sign	Feng Shui element
1970	Dog	Earth
1971	Pig	Water
1972	Rat	Water
1973	Ox	Earth
1974	Tiger	Wood
1975	Rabbit	Wood
1976	Dragon	Earth
1977	Snake	Fire
1978	Horse	Fire
1979	Goat	Earth
1980	Monkey	Metal
1981	Rooster	Metal
1982	Dog	Earth
1983	Pig	Water
1984	Rat	Water
1985	Ox	Earth
1986	Tiger	Wood
1987	Rabbit	Wood
1988	Dragon	Earth
1989	Snake	Fire
1990	Horse	Fire
1991	Goat	Earth
1992	Monkey	Metal
1993	Rooster	Metal
1994	Dog	Earth
1995	Pig	Water
1996	Rat	Water
1997	Ox	Earth
1998	Tiger	Wood
1999	Rabbit	Wood
2000	Dragon	Earth

Year	Chinese astrological sign	Feng Shui element
2001	Snake	Fire
2002	Horse	Fire
2003	Goat	Earth
2004	Monkey	Metal
2005	Rooster	Metal
2006	Dog	Earth
2007	Pig	Water
2008	Rat	Water
2009	Ox	Earth
2010	Tiger	Wood
2011	Rabbit	Wood
2012	Dragon	Earth
2013	Snake	Fire
2014	Horse	Fire
2015	Goat	Earth
2016	Monkey	Metal
2017	Rooster	Metal
2018	Dog	Earth
2019	Pig	Water
2020	Rat	Water

Colours and the elements

In Feng Shui the elements are related to individual colours which, again, are easily remembered by a Chinese analogy. This refers to the Feng Shui elements which you can look up in the pie charts in chapter 2.

Wood bears green colours; particularly for the Chinese, emerald green.

Fire colours are red, purple and orange.

Earth colours are the browns and yellows of loam and stone clays.

Metal colours are white or gold.

Water colours are blue and black.

Elemental colours in the home or office

An understanding of how the five elements and their colours interact together will help you to relate to Feng Shui; and to identify problems of imbalance which you can set about correcting. It can help in your selection of positive, helpful colour schemes.

You should choose colours which are compatible with, or better still supportive of, your own element. This is not your personal element – which influences personality and relationships – but your Feng Shui element – which concerns the Feng Shui principles relating to your home. For this purpose, you therefore need to look up the Feng Shui element relating to your year of birth in the pie charts (chapter 2). You will then be tapping into the qualities of the elements which will be most helpful for you personally.

When considering these colour issues, you must always refer to the pie chart for your Feng Shui element and remember the circle of compatibility. For example, say, from your pie chart you determine that your Feng Shui element is metal – a woman born in 1955, 1964 or 1982, or a man born in 1958, 1967 or 1976, for example. A predominance of white and gold room decorations – the colours of metal – will be compatible with your Feng Shui element. Browns and yellows – earth colours – will support and enhance your metal energy. But reds and oranges – fire colours – are not compatible. Blacks and blues – water colours – will reduce your sheen. Greens – wood colours – are neutral.

Elemental colours for clothing

Similarly, you can use the characteristics of the elements in your own clothing, to gain positive energy benefits. Again, this refers to the Feng Shui elements, not the astrological table. If your Feng Shui element is water, wearing an excess of wood colours – shades of green – will drain your energy because wood soaks up water. Similarly, too many earth colours – browns and yellows – will not be positive for you. On the other hand, metal would support your water element, so for an interview, for example, where you would like additional support, you should wear white or gold colours for metal with a touch of blue or black for your element.

Shapes and the elements

In the same way that the elements relate to specific colours, so they also relate to specific shapes. In this aspect of Feng Shui we are looking at the environment, the arrangement of buildings within it, the buildings themselves and for particular physical features and shapes. These shapes relate both to external shapes of buildings and the floor plan within those buildings.

Metal shapes are circular or crescent-shaped.

Water shapes include many gentle undulations.

Wood shapes are long, tall or L-shaped.

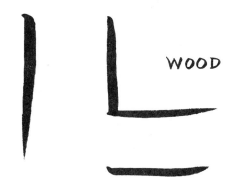

Fire shapes are triangular.

Earth shapes are square.

As shapes relate to specific physical or environmental features – for example, most houses are square or rectangular, many mountains tend to be triangular – so that physical feature is linked to a particular element. You will see how the pattern shows itself in the shapes of mountains. It can also be seen in the shape of houses. A square house will relate closely to the earth element, for example; a tall, thin house would relate more closely to wood.

A metal house

This is based on crescent shapes. A metal house is associated with money, so should be ideal for those who dabble in the markets, or for traders and business-minded people. All houses are influenced by 20-year cycles: rising good fortune followed by descending poor performance. For the inhabitants of the metal house, the rise in good fortune can be speedy during its 20-year span of prosperity, but after this there will be a marked downward trend and the house will have to be adjusted to counteract these affects. The 20-year cycles are described on page 53.

A water house

A house with numerous bays will, like the ebb and flow of the water, experience regular changes in fortunes – good to annoying and back again. Such inconsistency offers little promise of financial security while its influences are allowed to prevail.

A wood house

The long or rectangular-shaped house is stoic and reliable. Most houses benefit from this elemental association.

A fire house

A house influenced by the fire element will involve triangular shapes as part of its design, as in some chalet-style houses with very pointed eaves. As the flames of a fire leap up and down, so the health and financial situation of the family in a triangular house will fluctuate.

An earth house

Similar to the wood house, the square house offers security and stability.

CHAPTER 2

Your Birth Year

Sometimes the arrangement of a house may be very favourable for one occupant but not as favourable for the others. To maximise the positive elements of the situation and minimise the negative ones, organise your home according to your birth year, following the simple tables and pie charts in this chapter.

In this way you can determine which room directions are most appropriate for each individual and allocate these rooms as their bedrooms. Then Feng Shui the rest of the house in favour of the main breadwinner. Note that the calculations for a man differ from those for a woman. The tables repeat in a nine-year cycle.

Birth year direction tables

Year of Birth	Male	Female
1914	south-west	north
1915	south-east	south-west
1916	east	east
1917	south-west	south-east
1918	north	north-east
1919	south	north-west
1920	north-east	west
1921	west	north-east
1922	north-west	south
1923	south-west	north
1924	south-east	south-west
1925	east	east
1926	south-west	south-east
1927	north	north-east
1928	south	north-west
1929	north-east	west

Year of Birth	Male	Female
1930	west	north-east
1931	north-west	south
1932	south-west	north
1933	south-east	south-west
1934	east	east
1935	south-west	south-east
1936	north	north-east
1937	south	north-west
1938	north-east	west
1939	west	north-east
1940	north-west	south
1941	south-west	north
1942	south-east	south-west
1943	east	east
1944	south-west	south-east
1945	north	north-east
1946	south	north-west
1947	north-east	west
1948	west	north-east
1949	north-west	south
1950	south-west	north
1951	south-east	south-west
1952	east	east
1953	south-west	south-east
1954	north	north-east
1955	south	north-west
1956	north-east	west
1957	west	north-east
1958	north-west	south
1959	south-west	north
1960	south-east	south-west
1961	east	east
1962	south-west	south-east
1963	north	north-east
1964	south	north-west
1965	north-east	west

Year of Birth	Male	Female
1966	west	north-east
1967	north-west	south
1968	south-west	north
1969	south-east	south-west
1970	east	east
1971	south-west	south-east
1972	north	north-east
1973	south	north-west
1974	north-east	west
1975	west	north-east
1976	north-west	south
1977	south-west	north
1978	south-east	south-west
1979	east	east
1980	south-west	south-east
1981	north	north-east
1982	south	north-west
1983	north-east	west
1984	west	north-east
1985	north-west	south
1986	south-west	north
1987	south-east	south-west
1988	east	east
1989	south-west	south-east
1990	north	north-east
1991	south	north-west
1992	north-east	west
1993	west	north-east
1994	north-west	south
1995	south-west	north
1996	south-east	south-west
1997	east	east
1998	south-west	south-east
1999	north	north-east
2000	south	north-west
2001	north-east	west

Year of Birth	Male	Female
2002	west	north-east
2003	north-west	south
2004	south-west	north
2005	south-east	south-west
2006	east	east
2007	south-west	south-east
2008	north	north-east
2009	south	north-west
2010	north-east	west
2011	west	north-east
2012	north-west	south
2013	south-west	north
2014	south-east	south-west
2015	east	east
2016	south-west	south-east
2017	north	north-east
2018	south	north-west
2019	north-east	west
2020	west	north-east

Choosing the ideal site for your home

The pie charts on the following pages will show you how to choose the ideal position for your home and how the main rooms should be allocated to the individuals in the family. The numbers 1 to 4 represent the four beneficial winds. The letters A to D represent the four adverse influences. The symbols ⊥ and ↟ denote the ideal direction. Refer to the pie chart which relates to the direction for your year of birth.

The beneficial winds offer the following benefits:

1 Prosperous Wind denotes excellent financial position, health, vital energy.

2 Annual Progress denotes wealth, longevity and good health.

3 Good Doctor imparts speedy recovery from illnesses, a stable financial position and help and support from those around you.

4 Good Seat indicates that you will enjoy wealth, luck and health in an ordinary measure.

The corresponding four adverse influences have these effects:

A Bad Life denotes poverty, illness, sometimes even death.

B Five Ghosts indicates financial losses, poor health, and that you are easily jinxed.

C Six Bad Influences indicates that you are always jinxed, and have poor health and financial position.

D Disaster means that you are unable to retain money, are frequently involved in arguments and litigation and are shouted at regularly.

East, the direction of wood

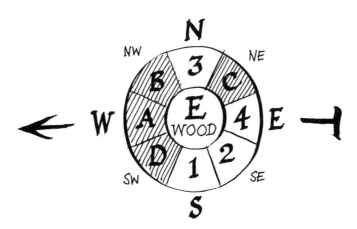

South-east, the direction of wood

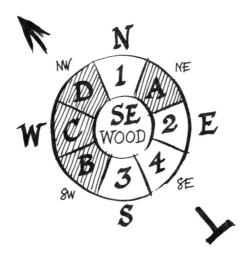

North, the direction of water

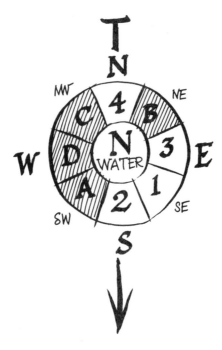

South, the direction of fire

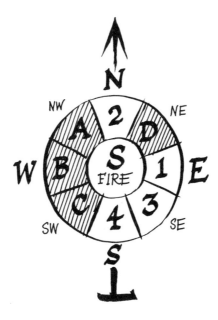

North-west, the direction of metal

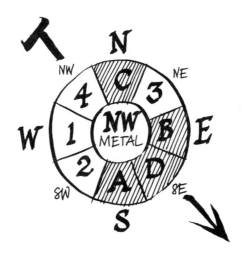

South-west, the direction of earth

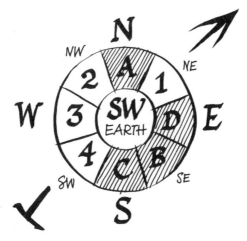

North-east, the direction of earth

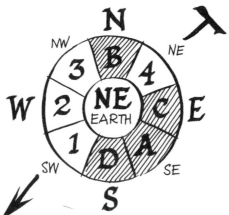

West, the direction of metal

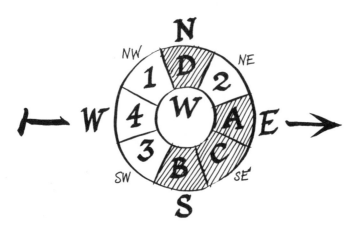

Maximising the possibilities

Not everyone's house will correspond to the suggested ideals; it is unlikely to be aligned in the most auspicious direction for the running 20-year cycle with doors correctly aligned for air, water and your personal direction (see pages 53, 47 and 19). So what you need to do is to make sure that your bed and your desk are correctly positioned. Your bed is your energiser where you wake up feeling lethargic or revitalised. Move your bed out of areas A, B, C or D and into sections 2, 3 or 4. Then you will be able to face the world with the best possible spirit.

Step by step calculations

Using the information in the birth tables and the pie charts on pages 19–26, you can make some simple calculations to determine the best direction for your house, and the most positive way to organise its internal and external features. By doing so you will harness positive forces and benefit your own life and the lives of those around you. These guidelines will repeat the process we have discussed so you have a quick reference.

Remember that the calculations differ for a man or a woman.

When you have made your calculations, Feng Shui the rest of the house in favour of the head of the house.

Step 1

Find your personal Feng Shui direction according to your year of birth (see pages 19–22).

Step 2

Find the pie chart that shows your personal direction in the inner circle (see pages 23–26).

Example of a woman born in 1958

For the year 1958, the personal Feng Shui direction for a woman is south, belonging to the element fire. (Note that this element is always found from the pie chart and does not relate to the personal element for her year of birth relating to her astrological sign.) Directions marked 1 to 4 show Beneficial Winds. Directions marked A to D illustrate Adverse Influences.

If house-hunting, the ideal direction for her house is with the main door facing north and the back of the house facing south. If she is already in a home, she should use as the main entrance, the door facing directions 1,2,3 or 4 in her personal pie chart.

Example of a man born in 1958

For the year 1958, the personal Feng Shui direction for a man is north-west, belonging to the element metal. Directions marked 1 to 4 show Beneficial Winds. Directions marked A to D illustrate Adverse Influences.

The ideal direction of this house is with the main door facing south-east and the back of the house facing north-west. Although the south-east quadrant is D, this is in fact okay as this is the ideal direction for a man born in 1958. For a good life, he should choose for his bedroom, a room with the door facing directions 1,2,3 or 4 on his pie chart.

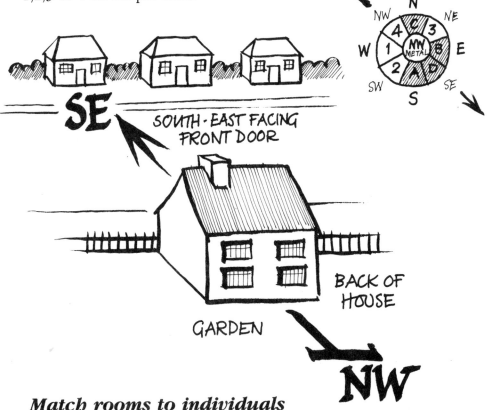

SOUTH·EAST FACING FRONT DOOR

SE

BACK OF HOUSE

GARDEN

NW

Match rooms to individuals

Within the house, ascertain which room directions are most appropriate for particular individuals. Place that individual's pie chart on a spot in the centre of the house. The directions marked 1 to 4 may be allocated as their bedroom.

Finally, Feng Shui the rest of the house in favour of the head of the house. Place their pie chart in the centre of all the other rooms in the house and Feng Shui from there.

CHAPTER 3

Yin and Yang: a Balance of Opposites

Yin and Yang – dark and light – are the two complementary principles of Chinese philosophy, the polar opposites of all existence. They exist as two sides of a coin. Yin is dark, feminine and negative. Yang is bright, masculine and positive. These complementary forces continually interact, creating change. Their interaction is thought to maintain the harmony of the universe and influence everything within it. Where they blend and achieve balance, there is harmony.

Yang elements include people, animals, light and artificial lighting.

Yin elements include houses, trees and dark, inanimate objects.

Balancing the dark influence of Yin with the light influence of Yang

Yin and Yang affect your home and the way you organise it. The following examples illustrate some common negative problems with houses, and offer suggestions for dealing with them.

The use of Yin and Yang here is so that your house is not too dark, because in Feng Shui it is said that 'if the sun does not visit your house, the doctor will'. Yin and Yang can be introduced in the landscape. For example, in a big garden, shrubs, rose arches and rockeries can have a pleasing effect on a flat landscape.

Heavy Yin influence

The situation

Even before entering a house, you can sometimes sense darkness – both physical and atmospheric – attributable to dense foliage, overgrown hedges or too close a proximity to woodland.

The effects

This has the effect of stifling the light of Yang and will create an unnecessary heaviness.

The solution

It will help to cut back the foliage that is the cause of the problem so that it has less of a negative effect. Up to a point, the more windows there are in the house the better. If the house is dark, introduce additional windows. If this is not possible, maximise the light available by having light curtains and hanging them beyond the edge of the window area when they are open.

Too many windows

The situation

A house can have too many windows to remain in balance.

The effects

This will have the effect of introducing too much light, making the occupants bad tempered. It will mean that air from all different directions is mixing together and disrupting the energy flow.

The solution

Simply keep some windows shut, or use curtains to dampen the lightening effect.

Satellite dishes

The situation

A main window or door looking out on to a round satellite dish opposite.

The effects

Energy will be lost from the house.

The solution

Use nets to shield the view, or break the outflow of energy by putting plants on the windowsill. You do not need to keep the curtains drawn.

Overlooking a washing line

The situation

Windows are facing somebody else's garden and looking at their washing line, which is closer than 30 metres (100 feet).

The effects

This gives too much Yin if the clothes are women's underwear. It has bad implications with relation to money running through your fingers.

The solution

Put curtains on either side of the window; you need not keep them drawn. Avoid the temptation to spend money unwisely.

The Green Dragon and the White Tiger

The Dragon relates to the left-hand side, symbolising power. The Tiger relates to the right-hand side, symbolising negative qualities. Just as you have two sides of the coin, light and dark, and so on, so one side of the house belongs to the Tiger and the other to the Dragon. You try to shift the balance in your favour by placing more things on the Dragon side to enhance power. In general, accentuate the positive influence of the Dragon by placing important items on the left-hand side of desks or the left-hand side of a room (as you enter through its main door), for example.

This influence can be shown in the position of your home in relation to other houses. Looking out from the door of the house, to the left, the predominating influence is of the Green Dragon, which is the masculine. Its feminine counterpart, the White Tiger, rules on the right-hand side.

If the houses to the right of your house stand taller or closer together, or there are more houses to the right than to the left, the White Tiger predominates. This indicates that the women of the house have greater influence. There is no need to try to aim for a perfect balance between these influences, but you may find the following examples amusing if you assess the likely circumstances of the houses you pass.

Strong Dragon influence

The Tiger is on the right of the house and these houses are smaller. The Dragon is on the left of the house and these houses are taller. The Tiger is lower than the Dragon, so the masculine influence predominates and the man is dominant. This situation is fine because the Dragon is a benevolent force.

A home with no Tiger

If a house has two houses on the left and none on the right, the male will be especially dominant. The house will have some luck, but it will come in a trickle because there is no Tiger. In Feng Shui, both should be present, but the Dragon must be more powerful.

Applying general Feng Shui principles to the house will have a positive influence.

Strong Tiger influence

There are three houses to the right and only one to the left. The influence of the Dragon is much less than the influence of the Tiger. Again the feminine influence is predominant and the female occupants will enjoy better luck than the men in the house.

Too much Tiger influence

If a house has a very large building to the right-hand side, the negative influence of the Tiger is great and the occupants will constantly argue amongst themselves. They can place a free-hanging piece of crystal on the bedroom window that looks directly on to the building to project dancing dots of sunlight on to the bedroom walls. Alternatively, place a dragon ornament on the left-hand side of the living room.

Evenly balanced house

A house is flanked on either side by houses of a similar size or taller, detached houses. Help is always close at hand.

Solitary house

A house standing alone is without help or support, and its occupants must therefore be self-reliant.

CHAPTER 4

The Physical World and Feng Shui

A ny house must relate to its physical surroundings, so let's look first at how specific homes relate to their environment.

As we said in the Introduction, Feng Shui simply means 'wind and water', and these are the two vital factors that influence the flow of energy through a house. Winds can be harsh or beneficial, and mountains offer shelter from less auspicious winds and useful vantage points. Water nourishes the soil. Ancient Chinese wisdom holds that the mountains control people and that water dictates the flow of money. The site chosen to build a new home would always be near and have the right relationship with both a mountain and water features. Traditionally, the Ancient Chinese would refuse outright to build a home where either of these factors was absent.

In Feng Shui today, such mountain and river features remain at its heart and are equally significant. However, our way of life has changed dramatically; few of us are lucky enough to live anywhere near either of these natural features. For most of us the relationship has become symbolic: mountains are represented by tall buildings, rivers by roads.

Mountains and buildings

In Feng Shui terminology, 'mountain' refers to a large structure or building within the immediate surroundings of a house. To be regarded symbolically as a mountain, the building should be larger than your own house. At ground level, it should also be higher than your home, although just a few centimetres higher will be good enough to classify it as a mountain.

On the other hand, if at ground level the land is just fractionally lower than your house, then it represents a river.

Mountains play a vital role in Feng Shui because they symbolise support, backing and positions of command. They can realise this support because they are higher and larger than your own house. The power that is derived from having such support is that the people in those buildings:

* do things for you;

* receive and accept your ideas readily;

* are able and willing to care for you.

Mountains behind a house therefore offer support and protection, and can also indicate that the inhabitants under this influence will attract wealth. It follows that a solitary house – one where the houses to its left and right are some distance away – is without such help and support, so the occupants must learn to be self-reliant or take the necessary steps open to them in Feng Shui.

A string of houses behind a house, rather than a single, larger building, is also favourable and is seen to offer continual support. But houses backing on to parks and open spaces will not find this external support, and to ensure success in their ventures the occupants will have to resort to Feng Shui to balance this situation.

House backed by parkland

The situation

A house has a park or large open space behind it, with no other larger buildings.

The effects

An open space behind the house means that the house loses the protective influence of a mountain in that position.

The solution

Add shrubs to the garden and erect a low fence along the border of the garden. This replaces the positive, protective influence that would be provided by the mountain. It provides a barrier, keeping the positive energies in the area of the house.

Mountain shapes and the elements

As you have already seen, in Feng Shui everything is classified into one of the five elements: wood, fire, earth, metal and water. So, working within this framework, we must also classify mountains. And, of course, you must remember that the elemental shapes relate not only to mountains but to their symbolic equivalents, buildings.

A wood mountain is slim and tall.

A fire mountain refers to a chain of angular, sharp ridges.

An earth mountain refers to a flat plateau shape.

A metal mountain refers to a gentle curve.

A water mountain refers to a series of gentle undulations.

WATER

With the exception of the fire mountain, the shapes all portend good luck, so there is no need to take any action to harness the supportive influence of the mountain. You will feel their influence on your house.

The fire mountain

The situation

The fire mountain, on the other hand, which has a jagged outline, has a negative influence. If the summit of the mountain is crowned with rocks, or buildings are jagged against the skyline – for example, adorned with aerials, neon signs or other sharp features – they constitute a fire mountain.

The effects

*The effect of this mountain behind a house will be to encourage
people to talk behind your back. You will be more likely to make
enemies and those in high positions will argue with you. Within
the family, skin problems and stomach ailments arise on an
unexpectedly regular basis and remain a constant threat. This
will be even more true if the house is south-facing and looks out
directly on to such a fire mountain. The occupants of such a
house may have the additional propensity to suffer from poor
eyesight or eye problems of some kind.*

The solution

**The solution is to hang net curtains to obscure the
mountains from view. Alternatively, you can deflect their
negative energy by fixing a round, convex mirror on to
the exterior wall to neutralise the negative features.**

Water and roads

Water is of profound importance in Feng Shui because in the
terminology of Feng Shui, water refers to one's financial situation.

Since few of us live near rivers, water is represented by roads
when we are looking at the Feng Shui situation of a house. A
ground level even a fraction lower than the house is representative
of a road and therefore of water. However, if there is water near
a house, then obviously this is very relevant to the assessment of
that house. Indeed, some people construct fountains in the
forecourts of their property in the hope of encouraging financial
gain. This only works for an east-facing house, until the year
2003. From 2004 it will apply to houses facing south-east (see
Tong Wan cycle, page 47).

The effect of the water or roads near the house is affected by the
relationship of the movement of the water to the elements, and
also by the position of the water in relation to the house.

Water and the elements

In the same way that the shapes of the mountains or buildings correspond to the five elements, so five different types of water relate to the elements and determine the influence on your finances. Relate these descriptions either to the movement of water, or to the flow of traffic or passers-by in front of your house.

Wood water undulates in long ripples. It indicates an inability to retain money.

Fire water creates triangular shapes in the eddies and flows of the water. It is a warning that spendthrifts will run into trouble.

Earth water is characterised by small groups of ripples. Again, this indicates that money will run through your hands.

Metal water creates little circular movements. This signifies rising wealth. A light swishing movement of water or intermittent traffic indicates that money will flow to you.

Water relating to the water element is also positive. Moving in little waves, it is conducive to the generation of wealth.

Water in relation to the house

You must not assume that it is always lucky to face water. Apart from the quality and general appearance of the water and therefore its relationship to the five elements, you also need to consider whether the water is Tong Wan. Tong Wan relates to the 20-year cycle of directional changes in energy meridians. Each 20-year time span, or Wan, bears a different direction. The prime and good directions are outlined in the charts on the following pages. Relating the current time span and the position of the water to your house will enable you to decide whether the influence of the water is auspicious. If the directional flow of water is auspicious for the current 20-year cycle, you will reap swift financial rewards. If it is not, then you will need to take appropriate action.

Tong Wan for water

These charts will show you the prime aspect for water and also the good aspect for water or roads near your house.

Years 1984–2003

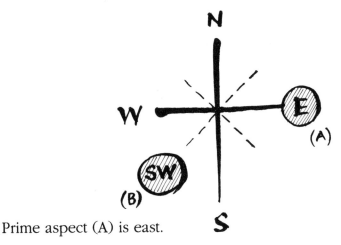

Prime aspect (A) is east.

Good aspect (B) is south-west.

Years 2004–2023

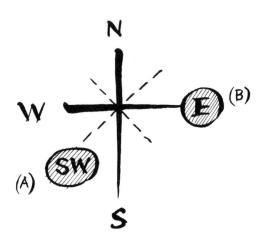

Prime aspect (A) is south-west.

Good aspect (B) is east.

Years 2024–2043

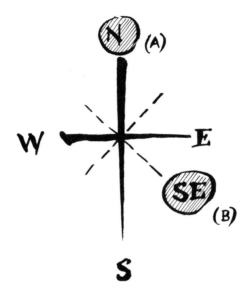

Prime aspect (A) is north.

Good aspect (B) is south-east.

Tong Wan water for 1997–2003

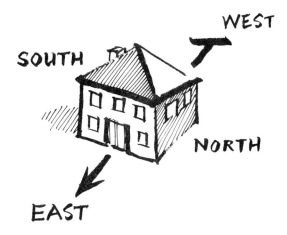

The situation

According to the chart, therefore, the prime aspect for water up to the year 2003 is east, so the ideal position is an east-facing house looking on to real water (not a street symbolising water).

This may explain your neighbours' enthusiastic commissioning of an ornamental fountain in their front garden on a date that coincides with the threshold of the next 20-year cycle.

The effects

In these circumstances, you will experience the Midas touch. Conversely, if the houses faces in the opposite direction – to the west – and looks out on to water, financial losses will be encouraged.

The solution

Consider how you can create a water feature in an appropriate eastern position for the prevailing Tong Wan.

Water quality

Having considered the direction and element of the water, you also need to consider its composition. The clearer and lighter the water, the stronger the positive financial influence on the fortunes of the home owner. If the flow of water or traffic on your street is both clear and light, money will come to you slowly but surely.

Even if the water or road is polluted and smells, provided it is Tong Wan the financial position will remain viable, although financial gains may come through dubious channels.

However, if the water or road is both polluted and is not Tong Wan, you will keep missing the correct strategies to generate wealth. Occupants will find themselves unable to keep their money, and will also suffer from poor health. Worse still, houses that look out on to noisy water or traffic are more likely to be plagued by financial losses and family dissension. If this is the case, hang nets to obscure the view and, if there is noisy traffic, take steps to reduce the noise by fitting double glazing, for example, or planting a hedge between the house and the road.

The shape of water

The shape of the water or road near your house will have an effect on the energies within the home. Occupants of houses in close proximity to an 's' bend enjoy prosperity, and a river or road encircling a house indicates a high propensity to make great savings.

House near a bend

The situation

A house situated on the dip of a pronounced bend of a river or a street is best avoided if you are buying a house; the river or street resembles a sickle.

The effects

The effects of this position can be equated with the erosion of wealth, an equivalent metaphor being that of a sickle hacking down opportunities. The sharper the bend, the stronger the negative influence.

The solution

The solution is to install a low gate between the front door and the road to act as a barrier and thereby to divert the negative energies. You could also construct a low fence or hedge.

Air

It is impossible to over-emphasise the fundamental importance of good air, and this means that the most important factor is the direction in which the house faces. Even if your house benefits from the advantageous positioning of favourable mountains or buildings and rivers or streets, the lack of good air will result in something like a 30 per cent reduction in your good fortune.

A generous space in front of a house is also conducive to the free flow of fresh air and its occupants will enjoy those little comforts that make life worth living. On the other hand, meagre space is a tell-tale sign of pressured, restless and nervous occupants.

There are three different types of air. Each type has an impact on your financial prospects, so is vital to your overall well-being.

Wong Hei air spells excellent wealth prospects.

Sang Hei air is thin and diluted. Progress only comes a slow step at a time.

Choon Hei air is ventilating. It is an improvement on Sang Hei air.

Tong Wan for air

'Wan' means the cycle, or time span. 1997 is in the 7th Wan, or 7th cycle. 'Tong Wan' means 'auspicious cycle'. This is linked with the Wan (or cycle) for water, discussed earlier.

Tong Wan refers to the auspicious direction in which your home should face. The perfect aspect, or Tong Wan, for the main door of your home is controlled by a 20-year cycle of directional changes in energy meridians. In Feng Shui, the fortunes of a house wax and wane with the relative advantages of a particular direction change. Referring to these directional changes, this table shows the best aspects depending on the year. Wong Hei represents the best aspects; Choon Hei a good aspect; Sang Hei is still fair. In other words, of the eight directions, these are the three best for each cycle.

Periods	Time span	Wong Hei (best aspect)	Choon Hei (good aspect)	Sang Hei (fair aspect)
1864–1883	1st Wan	north	south-west	east
1884–1903	2nd Wan	south-west	east	south-east
1904–1923	3rd Wan	east	south-east	central
1924–1943	4th Wan	south-east	central	north-west
1944–1963	5th Wan	east	north-east	west
1964–1983	6th Wan	north-west	west	north-east
1984–2003	7th Wan	west	north-east	south
2004–2023	8th Wan	north-east	south	north
2024–2043	9th Wan	south	north	south-west

Central means that the door direction is irrelevant as long as when you open the main door, air has easy access into the centre of the house.

Check the date of the purchase of your home against the chart. Suppose you bought a house in 1996. Note that 1996 accords with the 7th Wan in the chart. The direction most conducive to Feng Shui is for the house to be facing west; the next best is for the house to face north-east; the third best aspect is for the house to face south.

When you are purchasing property and are able to look to the long-term, you can reap additional benefits. For example, if you intend to retain the property for the next 40 years, it would be best to choose a property with a north-easterly aspect, as this overlaps with the 8th Wan. If you are looking even further ahead and want to purchase the property with a view to keeping it for the next 60 years, you would look for a southerly aspect. Although you have a few years in which the aspect is not optimum, you then have 20 years with a good aspect followed by 20 years with a prime aspect, as that direction follows through into the 8th and 9th Wan.

CHAPTER 5

The Link Between Houses and Roads

The position of houses and water or roads in relation to each other has significant effects on the well-being and fortunes of the occupants of those homes.

In the Introduction, we talked about the importance of Ch'i, the animating life-force in everything, which permeates our homes and other buildings, the physical landscape and surroundings, rivers, road, trees and, of course, people. Feng Shui enables you to tap the beneficial Ch'i energy to the maximum and disperse, disrupt or remove obstructions to its free flow.

Remember that in all the following examples, the purpose of the corrective measures is to increase receptivity, to focus and channel positive energy, or to deflect negative influences.

Ch'i energy is positive when, as a ventilating breeze, it is allowed to flow freely, lightly brushing everything it touches. Ch'i becomes negative energy when allowed to stagnate in dark nooks and crannies. It is positively harmful when channelled too quickly along straight paths, like a thunderbolt being hurled at your home.

With this image in mind, it follows that where your home is in a position which allows this negative thrust of energy, you need an effective buffer to divert that energy. In the case of Feng Shui, those buffers are symbolic. The most commonly used buffers are:

a round, convex mirror fixed above the front door to deflect such negative energy;

a low hedge, fence or gate introduced as a barrier;

the front door re-positioned in such a way that it opens away from, or at an angle, to the road running up to it.

You can apply whichever of these remedial measures seems most appropriate in your particular circumstances. Altering the position of a door, for example, may not be possible in your circumstances, and you would therefore have to adopt one of the other alternative solutions in order to facilitate the postive movement of energy.

The obstacles which you will confront are such things as chimneys, lamp posts, pylons, a cemetery and so on. They are only influential if they are less than 30 metres (100 feet) from the main door. Beyond that point they no longer affect the house. Their influence is greatest when they are directly in line with the main door; the impact is lessened the more the obstacle is angled away from the main front door. This is one reason why doors themselves may need to be repositioned at a new angle.

We have already looked at the road as representative of the river and its importance to the Feng Shui status of a house. Since so much in Feng Shui is symbolic and most of us no longer live near streams and rivers, as was so vital in ancient village communities, we look at roads as a representative of rivers in our modern urban environment.

House facing a T-junction

The situation

When a house is facing directly on to a T-junction, the suggestion is of a gun being pointed straight at the house. Quite clearly, this has a negative impact on the energies affecting the occupants of that house.

The effects

The occupants may suffer poor health and may seem accident-prone.

The solution

If it is possible, reposition the front door so that it opens at an angle which is not directly opposite the road, or move the door completely away from the road running up to it. Alternatively, introduce a low fence or hedge with a gate as a barrier to the negative energies. Another alternative is to place a mirror above the door to deflect the negative energies away from the house.

Road running up to the back

The situation

Where there is a road running directly towards the back of a house, the metaphor is of back-stabbing.

The effects

Petty talk will go on behind the back of the occupants. Even though they may be diligent and work hard, their promotion prospects are likely to be weak.

The solution

Place a mirror on a wall, gate or hedge at the back of the house where it will reflect the image of the road running up to it and thereby turn back the negative energies.

Road hitting a house at an angle

The situation

A road runs up to a house at an angle.

The effects

This will encourage money to drain away from the house. If the road is coming from the right-hand (or Tiger) side, the female occupants of the house will be accident-prone. If it is coming from the left-hand (or Dragon) side, the male occupants will be accident-prone.

The solution

Try to rehang the door so that it opens away from or at an angle to the road running up to it. Alternatively, have a low fence or hedge with a gate as a barrier against the negative effects. Place a mirror on the outside wall of the house to deflect the negative energies.

Two roads running up to a house

The situation

Two roads meet in front of a house, running up to it at an angle.

The effects

Both male and female occupants of the house will be exposed to ill-health and will find that they constantly bicker over financial matters.

The solution

Again, you should try to change the direction of the main door so that it opens at an angle away from the approaching roads. The aim is to avoid the road running directly up to the main door of the home. If this is not possible, place a mirror on the outside wall to deflect the energies away from the house, and construct a low fence or plant a hedge as a barrier against the negative energies.

Another option is to build a porch with an outer door to block the negative energy. Try to avoid leaving both doors open simultaneously.

House at a cross-roads

The situation

A house is positioned at a cross-roads or where roads fork. In both cases, there is a scissors effect, the negative energies cutting into the tranquillity of the home.

The effects

There will be a tendency towards minor accidents around the home.

The solution

Re-hang the door so that it opens at an angle away from the direction of the roads running up to it. Alternatively, introduce a low fence or hedge and gate as a barrier to this effect.

House at the dip of a crescent

The situation

A house is positioned at the dip of a crescent.

The effects

The occupants will experience financial instability, fortunes that continually rise and fall, and also, it is said, a tendency to cut themselves.

The solution

Introduce a low bush or gate between the front door and the apex of the curve.

House at the apex of a crescent, or near a raised motorway or railway line

The situation

A house is positioned with bedrooms on the same level as a raised motorway or railway line.

The effects

The occupants of this house will experience the increased likelihood of financial instability, rising and falling fortunes, and a tendency to cut themselves.

The solution

Place a convex mirror on the exterior wall to deflect the energies from the road or railway which is having these adverse effects on the occupants of the house.

House facing a busy road

The situation

A house is positioned alongside or facing a busy, fast-moving main road or motorway.

The effects

In this case, money will have a tendency to run away continuously and the occupants will find themselves unable to make savings.

The solution

Change the position of the front door, moving it to the side if possible. Failing this, create a barrier to keep the energy within the area of the house; for example, a gate, hedge or shrubs, or an outer porch. Or you could raise the threshold by two inches and place a mirror above the door to deflect the negative influences.

House at right angles to an L-shaped road

The situation

When a house is positioned squarely at a right-angle to an L-shaped road, the suggestion is of a knife cutting into the house.

The effects

The effects of this will be that the 'knife' cuts down both luck and money, with the occupants also being rather accident-prone.

The solution

Change the position of the front door, moving it to the side of the house if possible. Again, failing this create a barrier, such as a gate or hedge, to block the 'knife', or raise the threshold and place a mirror over the door.

Houses opposite an L-shaped road

The situation

Houses are positioned directly opposite an inverted L-shaped road.

The effects

The occupants of these houses seem to attract a regular stream of people overwhelmed with petty troubles.

The solution

Hang a convex mirror on the outside of the houses to deflect these minor problems. Alternatively, raise the thresholds slightly.

House surrounded by roads

The situation

A single house or a block of flats surrounded by roads so that it has a cross-roads at every corner.

The effects

This situation denotes money flowing out in different directions, and the occupants will find themselves unable to make savings.

The solution

Raise the threshold at the base of the door by 2.5 cm (1 inch) so that there is a raised threshold over which you must step to enter the house.

House near an S bend

The situation

A house is positioned near an S bend in a road.

The effects

The effects of this position are entirely positive. The occupants will enjoy prosperity and have great financial prospects

Houses on a circle

The situation

Houses form a semi-circle within the bend of a circle.

The effects

The occupants of all these houses will reap great financial gain. The best position, though, is at the apex of the circle.

Houses on a roundabout

The situation

Houses are positioned near the junctions of a roundabout.

The effects

This relates to an uninterrupted flow of water, hence money comes easily to these properties. Needless to say, this is a good Feng Shui position for a home as the financial energies are positive.

Corner facing the bedroom

The situation

The corner of the house opposite points directly at a bedroom window of a house.

The effects

The occupants of that bedroom will suffer ill-health.

The solution

Keep the curtains drawn when you're in the room, or put up net curtains. Change the use of that room from a bedroom. The bedroom is important because it is the place where we renew and gain strength for our everyday lives. It may not be so vital that other rooms have such a good Feng Shui aspect.

House facing a gap

The situation

A house is directly facing a tall, narrow gap between the
houses on the opposite side of the road.

The effects

*The occupants of the house may find that they are generally
accident-prone, not very energetic and not always in the best of
health.*

The solution

**Deflect the negative energies by positioning a convex
mirror on the front of the house to reflect the image
of the gap. You can also raise the threshold by 5 cm
(2 inches) so that you have to step over the threshold
to enter the house; this will act as a barrier to the
incoming negative energies.**

House facing an extension

The situation

The wing of a house or the extension of a building opposite points directly at the main door of the house.

The effects

This energy is bad for the heart and needs attention.

The solution

Place six gold-coloured coins under the threshold of the main door, heads side up, in a line parallel with the door. Or place a convex mirror on the outside of the house to reflect back the negative energy.

Corner opposite facing the house

The situation

The corner of the house opposite is aimed directly at a house.

The effects

This energy is bad for the heart and needs attention.

The solution

Deflect the negative energies using a convex mirror placed on the outside of the house so that it catches and throws back the reflection of the angle.

Triangular features

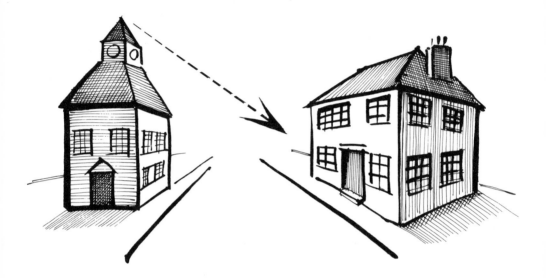

The situation

A triangular feature on the house opposite faces a front door of a house or the bedroom window.

The effects

The occupants of that bedroom or house will have a tendency to be accident-prone.

The solution

Hang net curtains in the affected bedroom window to act as a protective barrier.

House facing a round feature

The situation

A house has its main door directly opposite a round feature or dome on a building on the opposite side of the street.

The effects

The children in such houses will have a tendency to be unsettled and naughty.

The solution

Make sure that children's bedrooms do not look out over the dome. Parents, for example, could use those bedrooms as dome features do not affect adults. Alternatively, if there is enough space, use the rooms as playrooms or studies.

House opposite a gateway

The situation

A house is directly opposite a gateway, especially into a mews.

The effects

The general health of those living in the house will be affected, and they are likely to find that they are unable to achieve their full potential at work.

The solution

Change the position of the front door so that it does not open opposite the gateway. If this is not possible, place a convex mirror on the outside of the house to deflect the negative energies away from the house and create a more constructive Feng Shui situation.

House facing pylons

The situation

A house is positioned immediately opposite an electricity pylon.

The effects

This will cause the occupants to be susceptible to illness and minor fire accidents in the house.

The solution

Deflect the negative energies using an octagonal mirror placed above the front door so that it catches the reflection of the pylon and throws it back away from the house.

House opposite a cemetery

The situation

A property overlooks a cemetery, hospital or funeral parlour.

The effects

The occupants of such a house will be dogged by a series of unspecified illnesses and will be susceptible to fitful sleep.

The solution

Leave one small, low voltage light switched on in the house both night and day.

House facing a very large building

The situation

A house is positioned opposite a very large building.

The effects

Those who live in such a house often fall victim to fraud.

The solution

Defend yourself from such influences by making a rule not to lend money, by screening the view with net curtains, or by hanging a convex mirror over the main door.

House facing a church

The situation

A house is directly opposite a church.

The effects

This influence can render the occupants of the house quick-tempered and also create the feeling of being rather lonely.

The solution

Place a convex mirror on the outside of the building to deflect any negative energies.

House facing a lamp post

The situation

There is a lamp post directly in line with the front door of a house.

The effects

This can lead to ill-health and also encourage difficulties with the law or the courts.

The solution

Deflect the negative energies using a convex mirror on the outside of the house to catch and turn back the reflection of the lamp post.

House facing a tree

The situation

A house has a tree on the opposite side of the road, directly in line with the front door.

The effects

As with the lamp post, this can also encourage ill-health and the possibility of problems with the law or the courts.

The solution

Deflect the negative energies using a convex mirror on the ouside of the house to reflect the image of the tree and deflect its associated negative energies.

CHAPTER 6

The All-important Main Door

In Feng Shui, the aspect of the main door of a house is of cardinal importance because this is the entrance that lets in or keeps out the vital energy that promotes health, wealth and luck. Special emphasis is placed on the main door since all occupants pass through this entrance many times daily. Tradesmen, the postman, even strangers, come to the door.

The best position for the main door is usually in the middle of the house. In the UK, with a proliferation of semi-detached and terraced properties, this is not generally the situation. However, provided your house faces the correct direction for the relevant time span, your good luck will override anything. It then becomes immaterial whether your front door is positioned in the middle of the house or to one side.

If the door is not in the best position, and there is no suitable alternative entrance, create as much space as possible in front of it and keep the area uncluttered. You can also paint your front door in the colour that relates to the direction the door is facing; wood or fire colours if the front door is south facing, for example (see page 15).

In addition you can personalise your assessment for the best direction of the house in relation to the year of your birth, as you will see on pages 22–26.

Air

The air that enters the house through this crucial main door must be Tong Wan, that is, it must come from an auspicious direction, as we have already seen in previous chapters. So it is important that your main door is Tong Wan – that it faces the direction that is most auspicious for that particular time-cycle to enable it effectively to receive Wang Hei, Sang Hei or Choon Hei air. You will find full information on this on pages 52–53.

For 1997, you will see that the Tong Wan for air is west. So until 2003, the best aspect for the main door is with the back to the east and the front door facing the west.

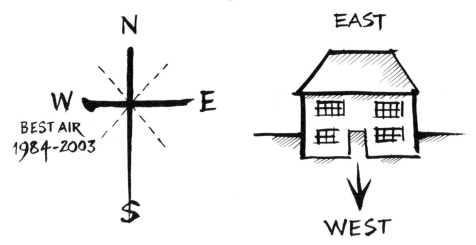

Let the Dragon and Tiger breathe

The situation

It is best if the main door does not conflict with the direction of the traffic. So as the traffic is moving past the house, the main door should ideally be on the end of the house which the traffic passes last. If there is a large space to the front of the house with a depth of at least 10 metres (30 feet) then it makes no difference where the door is located, since the space negates the effect of the traffic flow.

The effects

There are no ill effects, but if the door position 'flows' with the traffic, the occupants are able to generate more income.

The solution

Again, clear as much space as you can between the front door and the road. Failing this, place six brass coins in a line under the carpet just inside the door.

Space in front of the house

The situation

We have already seen that a park, garden or similar large space to the front of the house is beneficial, being conducive to the

free flow of air. A water feature such as a fountain in the
garden is particularly good, although only until 2003, and only
if the garden is east-facing.

The effects

*Having such a space will make the life of the occupants less
pressured and they will enjoy the ordinary things in life. A
cramped space indicates nervousness and restlessness. Such a
space will also balance any negative energies created by an
otherwise inauspicious traffic or water flow.*

The solution

**This arrangment is already very auspicious, but also
introduce a water feature such as a fountain, if possible,
in front of the house if it faces east. Even something
fairly small, such as a bird bath, will help to make the
most of the positive Ch'i.**

Toilet near the main door

The situation

Symbolically speaking, toilet air is 'stagnant' – it is air that you
don't want to have circulating around the house. Conversely,
kitchen air is 'live' and clashes with stagnant air. The main door
of the house is immediately opposite to the toilet door, or the
toilet door is immediately opposite the kitchen door.

The effect

*If there is a toilet directly opposite the main door, wealth will
constantly be flushed away from the house. If the kitchen and
toilet doors are opposite, there will be a clash of Yin and Yang.*

The solution

Place a screen before the toilet door or make sure that

you keep the toilet door closed so that it is not immediately seen as you enter. Use the same remedial measure where the kitchen and toilet doors are positioned exactly opposite each other.

Windows each side of the door

The situation

The main door of the house has windows on either side.

The effects

If your financial situation is bad, it may also be attributed to winds of good luck being dragged out through the windows on either side of the main door.

The solution

Place hardy, round-leafed plants on the windowsills to confine your luck within the house. If the sills are too narrow, you can hang the plants in containers in front of the windows.

A human look

The situation

The main door resembles the mouth of a human face and so
has a significant overall bearing on the Feng Shui of the house.

The Japanese also set great store by such factors, even if
intuitively. Part of their design research on cars focuses on the
overall impact of the radiators. Market research has shown that
models with radiators resembling down-turned mouths hold
little appeal, being deemed depressing.

The effects

*If the main door gives the visual impression of being down-
turned, the effect is depressing to the occupants of the house. It
may also have a negative effect on the financial circumstances
of those living there.*

The solution

**If possible, replace your front door with a more cheerful
design. Failing this, alter any features such as windows
or hinges to improve the look. You could paint the door a
more cheerful colour, but make sure it's compatible with
the element relevant to its direction (see below).**

The main door and the elements

We have already looked at the important relationship between
Feng Shui and the elements, the interaction of the earth, sun, sky,
moon, stars. It is important in Feng Shui to harmonise the basic
shapes, aspects and colours of the elements – metal, wood, earth,
fire and water – both with the elements of the occupants and
with the exterior and interior decor.

In Feng Shui, there are eight compass positions: north, south,
east, west, north-east, north-west, south-east, south-west. These

accord with the five elements. To discover how your main door relates to its elemental aspect, stand at the door, facing the street.

The relationship of main door aspect and elements

Door facing	Belongs to
East or south-east	Wood
South	Fire
South-west or north-east	Earth
West or north-west	Metal
North	Water

Main doors facing east or south-east

The best colours are those of wood (green) or water (black or blue).

Avoid the colours of metal (white or gold) or fire (red, purple or orange).

The colours of earth (brown or yellow) are neutral.

Main doors facing south

The best colours are those of wood (green) or fire (red, purple or orange).

Avoid the colours of water (blue or black) and earth (brown or yellow).

The colours of metal (white or gold) are neutral.

Main doors facing south-west or north-east

The best colours are those of fire (red, purple or orange) or earth (brown or yellow).

Avoid the colours of wood (green) and metal (white or gold).

The colours of water (black or blue) are neutral.

Main doors facing north

The best colours are those of metal (white or gold) or water (black or blue).

Avoid the colours of earth (brown or yellow) and wood (green).

The colours of fire (red, purple or orange) are neutral.

Wrongly assigned main door colours

The situation

The main door of a house is north-facing, therefore belongs to the element water. However, the colour of both the door and the doormat is green, the colour of the element wood.

The effects

Wood soaks up water, detracting from the luck of the occupants passing daily through the door. The north aspect is also the direction for the son of the household, based on his time and date of birth, and the effect is that he has not been doing well at school and is always ill.

The solution

The door should be painted white or gold, the colours of the element metal, and the green doormat replaced with a blue or black one, the colours of the element water. These colours of metal and water should support his water element and solve his problems.

Door patterns and the elements

Once you become acquainted with the interaction of the five elements, you will be better able to choose the main door patterns that are supportive for your home. These patterns can be utilised in the shapes of the wooden structure of the door itself – the panels in its construction. Or they can be patterns in the glazing – a semi-circular window in the door, for example.

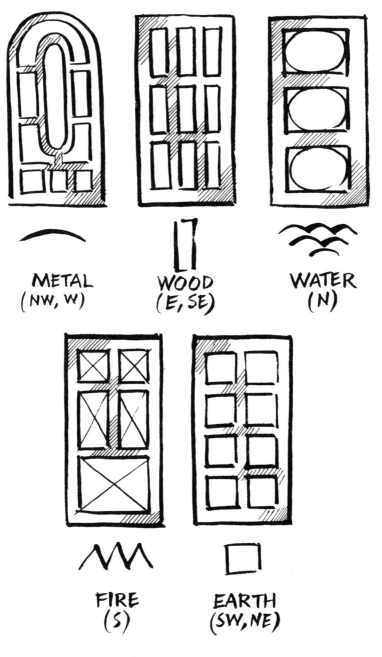

METAL
(NW, W)

WOOD
(E, SE)

WATER
(N)

FIRE
(S)

EARTH
(SW, NE)

East or south-east aspect

The long, rectangular shapes of wood.

South aspect

The triangular shapes of fire.

South-west or north-east aspect

The square shapes of earth.

West or north-west aspect

The crescent shapes of metal.

North aspect

The undulating or repetitive circular shapes of water.

Door positions

Where the door is positioned in relation to other features can also affect the Feng Shui of a house and should be considered alongside the other aspects of direction, relationship to the road, the elements, and so on.

Because the main door is so crucial to the well-being of the house, it is important to consider the door in all its aspects. Look at what is immediately opposite the main door.

Eaves facing a main door

The situation

The eaves of the roof across the road from the lady's house are pointing directly at her front door. The position of the front door is in the south-east, which is also the personal direction of the lady occupant. The eaves have a triangular, fire shape and are therefore not compatible with the south-easterly direction of the door, which links to the element wood.

The effects

The lady notices that the washing machine and other electrical appliances keep breaking down. She herself seems to have become prone to falls.

The solution

Hanging a set of 'keiloon' or chimera on the inside of the front door (see page 98) and also placing a round convex mirror on the outside above the front door would push the negativity away into the distance, thereby minimising its effect.

Main door at the foot of stairs

RAISED THRESHOLD

The situation

The front door of a house or flat is at the foot of a flight of
stairs and stands opposite the stairs.

The effects

*The occupants of the house are likely to suffer generally poor
health and lack of energy.*

The solution

**Raise the threshold beneath the door by about 5 cm
(2 in) from the floor so that you step over the threshold
into the house.**

Main door at the top of stairs

SMALL CONCAVE
MIRROR

The situation

The main door of a house or flat is at the top of a flight of
stairs and directly in front of them.

The effects

*Money will roll straight out of the front door of the home and
down the stairs. The occupants will find it difficult to hang on to
the fruits of their labours.*

The solution

Place a concave mirror above the door on the outside of the home. This pulls in the money and keeps it inside the house.

Door opposite a lift

The situation

The main door of a home, most usually an apartment or flat, is directly opposite a lift and the lift doors are repeatedly opening and shutting.

The effects

This adversely affects the fate and fortune of occupants of the home.

The solution

Place a convex mirror above the door on the outside of the home to deflect the influence of the lift, and raise the threshold beneath the door by 5 cm (2 in) so that you step over the threshold into the house.

Too many doors

The situation

In some houses, particularly large ones, there may be too many openings to contain the circulating Ch'i, or life-force.

The effects

If the Ch'i is not contained, the home will not feel its positive benefits.

The solution

It is best to leave only a maximum of five doors ajar and keep any other doors (such as the bedrooms, toilets or kitchen) closed when not in use.

Other features of doors

Indoor arches are for temples and churches. In family homes, they do not promote health and intimacy. On the contrary, they generate petty arguments within the household and undermine health.

Arched door shapes belong to the element metal, and for the 20-year time span until 2003, metal lies in the west, and therefore arcs bear no adverse effects. However, from the year 2004 onwards, arched doors in family homes will not be desirable features.

CHAPTER 7

Inside your Home

In the same way that you have applied the principles of Feng Shui to the locality and aspect of your home, so you can also position your furniture and organise your interior decor to maximise positive influences and minimise negative aspects. The balance of Yin and Yang and the colours associated with the elements are important here. The aim is for harmony and balance which can be achieved through strategic positioning of objects and the use of colour and light.

Arranging your rooms

To arrange interiors, stand in the middle of each room and face its main door.

On your left is the powerful Dragon, on your right lies the sleeping Tiger. Place things in constant use – such as the clock, electrical equipment, radiator and computers – more to the left half because the left belongs to the Dragon, the positive symbol of power. The opposite half of the room, belonging to the sleeping Tiger, must be kept quiet, calm and static.

From this position in the middle of the room you will also need to establish the quadrants of the room as they relate to the points of the compass.

These quadrants of the room also relate to the elements. The west and north-west section of the room belongs to metal, the east and south-east belong to wood. The south belongs to fire and the north to water. The north-east and the south-west belong to earth.

The hall

In Feng Shui, the space between the floor and the ceiling is split into three equidistant, symbolic levels: the earth, the human and the sky.

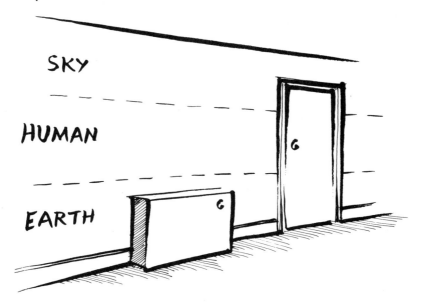

Items symbolic of those levels should be placed in the relevant position. For example, a shoe rack by the entrance, on the same wall as the main door, should not be higher than the bottom third of the hall. Shoes collect earth, so if the shoe rack comes up to human level, this will affect the health of the household.

Wind chimes on the main door invite evil if the door is in the north-east or south-west direction. Avoid placing them there.

The keiloon, or chimera, is a legendary creature with horns on the head of a lion, scales on the body of a deer and the tail of a serpent. Legend has it that this creature eats wicked people. Tricksters, thieves and murderers should not hang the keiloon by their door as they themselves will be 'eaten'. Placed at the front door with its mouth facing the door, the keiloon is the sentinel that neutralises any harmful elements entering, and has a health-giving effect upon the house. If the Feng Shui positioning of a house is unfavourable, the keiloon will dilute any diverse energies circulating around the house.

The living room

Because the living room is the place where the occupants gather, the atmosphere is thick with Yang. Clocks, televisions, air-conditioning and radiators exert a pervasive effect as they are constantly in use.

The living room belongs to the element metal. Having a round clock in gold or white (not silver or chrome) hanging in the west or north-west section of the living room will impart very good luck to the family. The best position generally for clocks is to the left side of the room and, if possible on the same wall as the main door into the room.

Paintings for the living room

Follow the advice below to ensure that the paintings in your living room maximise the positive influences.

Images of swimming fish denote longevity.

Lambs are symbolic of light and brightness and hence luck.

Landscapes are good if they depict morning sunrise, mountains or water. Sunsets induce lethargy and end-of-life feelings.

Cascading water induces good luck for the household.

Portraits are best if they are showing relaxed and smiling faces. Large portraits of deceased members of the family evoke too much nostalgia. You want to celebrate life and encourage positive, forward-looking feelings.

Large paintings with excessively dark or vivid colours, or those depicting vicious wild beasts induce poor health.

Paintings based on geometric shapes, using a very limited range of colours, arouse destructive instincts.

Paintings which are excessively red in colour will encourage irritability within the household.

Plants for the living room

Most plants or flowers are good Feng Shui in the living room as long as they are not wilting and have no dead flower heads. However, plants with spiky, sharp leaves denote poor health. So if you keep cacti, beware! In particular, avoid keeping them in the kitchen, which is associated with health. Plastic or artificial plants are neutral; they do not affect Feng Shui. You are therefore best to select softer foliage plants.

Carpets in the living room

If large rugs or carpets are predominantly red, avoid the north-west section of the living room, as this belongs to metal. Red is the colour of fire and melts metal. This also applies to large paintings over 1.25 metres (4 feet) in size. The east and south-east belong to wood so should also be avoided for large red-dominated rugs or pictures as fire burns wood. Neutral positions are south – which belongs to fire – and north – which belongs to water and therefore holds water in check. In general, choose rugs in colours that are appropriate to the element of the part of the rooms you are placing them in. Carpets that cover the whole of the room should suit the direction of the room itself: if it is in the south-east part of the house, for example, choose wood colours such as greens.

Ornaments

Souvenirs or ornaments made of metal need to be positioned strategically if they are not to attract adverse influences. The north-west section of the living room belongs to metal. Excessive metal leads to a tendency for members of the family to suffer minor injuries to limbs. Placing some of the metal objects in the neutral sections of the room, east or south-east, will minimise the adverse influence.

Pets

Cats belong to the element wood, so the colours for their blankets should be the blues or black of water or the greens of wood. Red is a very bad choice for cats' bedding. Front doors opening to the north-east, south and north-west make cats very strong and healthy. The north and south-west do not make good openings for cats.

Dogs belong to the element earth. Metal detracts from earth, so white baskets make dogs ill. Choose browns or yellows. Main doors opening into the south-west, north-east or south make a dog strong, whilst those facing south-east and east make it feel poorly.

The kitchen

The kitchen is associated with health. As the place where nourishment is prepared, the kitchen affects our internal composition and therefore the general well-being of the family.

The strategic positioning of cooking appliances can reduce, obstruct or even induce the free flow of energies.

A window opposite the kitchen door is fine, but electrical appliances which are in constant use, and the boiler, are best placed on the left-hand side of the room.

The best position for the kitchen

The kitchen belongs to the element fire. The north section of the house belongs to water, the east and south-east belong to wood. Since fire requires water for cooking and wood keeps the fire burning, assign your kitchen to the north, east or south-east section of the house. The north-east belongs to the element earth, which is neutral. The south-west, on the other hand, is not a good position for the kitchen.

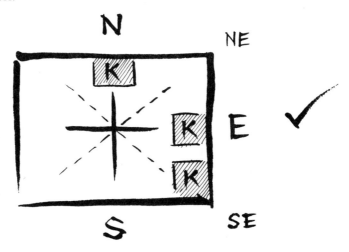

If a kitchen in 1997 faces south-west, with its hob or cooker also situated in the south-west section of the room this is the worst position in this 20-year cycle. It will have the effect of making the occupants suffer digestive disorders. The solution is to move the cooker to any other part of the kitchen. Position a small mirror so that it catches the reflection of the cooker and reflects it into another corner of the kitchen.

The cooker

Shelves must be at least 1 metre (3 feet) above the cooker to avoid having a detrimental effect on the family's health. If necessary, remove any shelves that are too close to the cooker. Shelves to the side of the cooker are not affected.

A sink tap pointing to a cooker gives rise to stomach upsets. Either put an ornament or a piece of furniture between the tap and the cooker, or place a mirror above the cooker to reflect back the energy.

Water pipes can run under the cooker but not under the floor just below the cooker.

The fridge

Turn the fridge doors and the cooker doors away from the kitchen door. The fridge should not open facing the kitchen door. Fridge is Yin and clashes with people walking in because people are Yang. Further more, the fridge doors should not stand directly opposite the cooker, as cold from the fridge and fire from the cooker do not mix. It should be possible to rehang your fridge door so it hinges away from the door and the cooker.

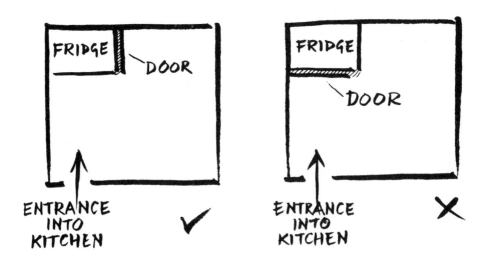

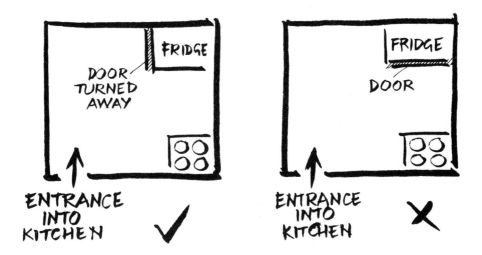

The sink

The best position for the sink during the present 20-year cycle is east, as the direction for water is east. The next best is the south-west. Water symbolises money, so a sink to the west is money down the drain. If you cannot reposition a badly-placed sink, generally make sure that the area around the sink is dry when not in use. Always fix leaky tap washers promptly. Avoid leaving dishes soaking in the sink. If you have to leave glasses or mugs around the sink to wash later, first tip out the water in them.

The dining room

Dining tables should not be placed directly in front of the main door. A dining table facing the toilet door receives too much Yin and can affect health. The use of a dining table as a partition between two rooms is not recommended. If a dining table faces the kitchen, or is in the kitchen area, it absorbs too much Yang and will give diners a bad temperament.

Air-conditioning, central heating and fans are best on the left-hand side of the dining room.

The bedroom

The bedroom is associated with rest, relaxation, comfort and licence to behave freely, and about eight hours are spent in bed each day, so it is a very important room. If a person is not sufficiently rested, they will not perform to their best abilities and will not be able to take advantage of the good fortune released into the rest of the house. It follows therefore that beds, lights, wardrobes and dressing tables make a contribution to a harmonious atmosphere.

It is best if you can personalise the position of your bed according to the direction calculated from the year of your birth. Refer to pages 19–26. If you share a bed, find the most compatible direction for the two of you.

The bedroom door

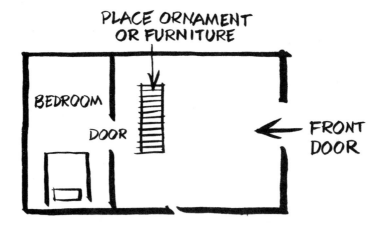

If the main door of the flat or house stands directly opposite the bedroom door, the occupant of that bedroom will be prone to legal problems. Position a small ornament or piece of furniture to interrupt the line of passage, the flow of Ch'i, from the main door to the bedroom.

Bed headboards

You can tap into the strengths of the elements by choosing a headboard with a shape relating to a particular element. Remember to consider the compatibility cycle in the relation to the elements (see page 8) in relation to your own Feng Shui element when you are making your choice. Look up your pie chart. Suppose the inner circle says 'wood', then that is the shape for you. The headboard shape itself is not vital. What is really important is positioning the bed in the correct quadrant 1,2,3 or 4 in the pie chart.

Metal-shaped headboards

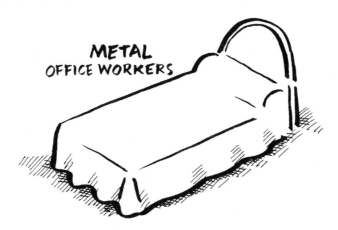

In Feng Shui, a round or arc-shaped headboard belongs to the element metal. It is a good shape to choose, especially if you work in an office or are involved with paperwork and if your personal basic element is metal, for then you have Feng Shui in double strength.

Wood- and earth-shaped headboards

Square or rectangular headboards belong to the elements wood and earth and are good for professional people, encouraging stability and offering support.

Water-shaped headboards

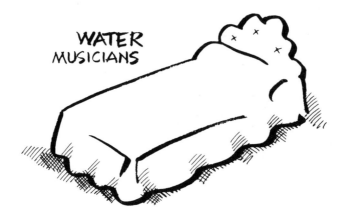

Oval or wavy forms belong to the element water and are best for artists, musicians and designers.

Fire-shaped headboards

Angular headboards are not recommended for anyone. They relate to the element fire, and are only good for those who never need to sleep!

Bunk beds

The head of the person on the top bunk must not touch the ceiling when they sit up in bed, otherwise they will suffer from poor health. The tops of the mattresses are best at least 40 cm (16 in) off the ground.

Clocks

It is not good Feng Shui to place a clock immediately behind or directly in front of a sleeper. Place clocks on either side of the bed, but not by the middle section of the bed.

Light bulbs

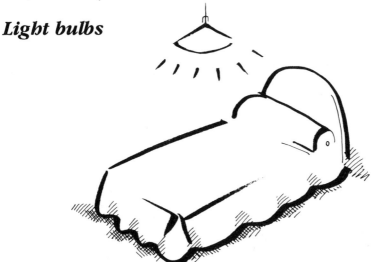

A light bulb directly above the head of the bed will turn the sleeper into a nervous wreck. If hung above the centre of the bed, it will cause stomach disorders. Instead, the light should be placed to the side of the bed.

Bed near a chimney breast

When beds are pushed into chimney breasts, or there is a mantelpiece above the headboard, success will elude the sleeper as this creates pressure on the sleeper. To counteract this, place six gold or brass coins on each side of the mantelpiece.

Dressing tables

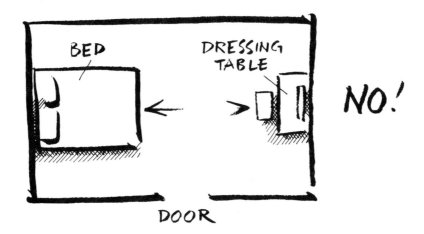

Dressing tables placed at the foot of the bed will adversely affect health. Move the dressing table to any other position.

Desks

Desks are associated with career, and need to be well set up to take advantage of the positive.

Desk positions

If you position a desk directly opposite and facing the door, it will adversely affect breathing and concentration.

Sitting too close to a door with one's back to the door will affect exam performance.

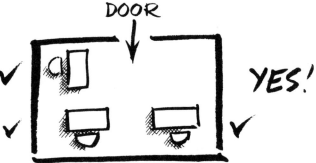

Sit with your back to a wall with the desk in a corner; this is a good position for a desk.

The optimum position for a desk is the position of the star that rules mental activities, and this position moves annually, so the best positions for the desk are in the relevant quadrant of the room: 1995 south-east; 1996 centre; 1997 north-west; 1998 west; 1999 north-east; 2000 south; 2001 north.

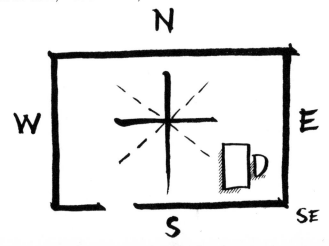

Other points relating to desks

Cabinets and shelves above desks, if built in as part of the whole unit, are acceptable, but otherwise shelves above the desk create pressure upon the person at the desk.

Supporting beams above desks will create pressure or tiredness.

A light directly above the head numbs concentration.

It is not good to sit where you will obstruct a doorway.

Do not sit too close to a window.

Clocks should also not be placed in front of writing desks. The person sitting at the desk should not have the clock face directly in front of them.

It is particularly important that office chairs are the right elemental colour so that you gain the positive effects of the colour. Choose a colour that suits your own element, checking this against the pie chart on pages 23–26 which relates to your Feng Shui element, not your personal astrological element.

Metal people should choose brown or white to gain support or strength from earth or metal.

Water people should choose white or blue to gain strength or understanding from metal or water.

Wood people should choose blue or green to gain understanding or co-operation from water or wood.

Fire people should choose green or red to gain co-operation or dynamism from wood or fire.

Earth people should choose red or brown to gain dynamism or support from fire or earth.

CHAPTER 8

Feng Shui and the Family

The internal organisation of the home – the placing of furnishings and its colour schemes – are vital in promoting the positive and inducing harmony. There are traditional directions and colours associated with the ages and roles of the various members of the family. Particular areas of the home are traditionally allied to age ranges and genders within the family, and special colours are associated with those groups. These are independent of the personal and Feng Shui element colours related to those people because of their birth sign.

Who goes where?

The south-west belongs to the mother and women aged 46 and over.

The north-west belongs to the father and men aged 46 and over.

The east is reserved for the eldest son and men in the household aged 31 to 45 years.

The south-east is for the eldest daughter and women in the household aged 31 to 45 years.

The south is for women aged 16 to 30 years.

The north belongs to men aged 16 to 30.

The west belongs to girls aged one to 15.

The north-east belongs to boys aged one to 15.

Use the power of colour

The use of colour schemes in interior decoration is an effective tool in Feng Shui. The use of colour may support or detract from the energies associated with a certain area, and sometimes adjustments in the placing of furniture or other household items may help individuals deal with problems they may be experiencing.

Colour is a powerful tool. Use it in the home to maximise the positive energies of individuals. The following information will show you the traditional links between individuals and particular colours. The colours can be used in any items of decoration such as rugs, wallpaper, carpets or mats. You only need an overall predominance of the appropriate colour.

Colours in the east and south-east

The east is reserved for the eldest son and men aged 31 to 45, the south-east for the eldest daughter and women aged 31 to 45. Blue and black items of decoration – water colours – placed in these areas in the home enhance the energies of these individuals. Keep red fire colours in these sections to a minimum.

Colours in the south

The south is for women aged 16 to 30. The fire colours of red, orange and purple are the best, while water colours, blacks and blues, are best avoided.

Colours in the south-west and north-east

The south-west is for the mother and women aged over 46, while the north-east is for boys up to the age of 15. Introduce the browns and yellows of earth colours. Predominantly white or gold, metal colours are undesirable.

Colours in the west and north-west

The west is for girls under 15 and the north-west for the father and men over 46. Beneficial colours are the metal whites and golds. Avoid a predominance of the fire colours red, orange and purple.

Colours in the north

This area is for men aged 16 to 30. Support colours are metal white and gold. Avoid earth browns and yellows.

Remedial colours

Now and then a member of the family may be going through a spell of bad luck or poor health. To help concentrate their energies, find the areas within the house specific to them and balance the Feng Shui. For example, if the eldest son deals on the stock exchange, move red-coloured carpets away from the east section of the rooms he spends most time in.

An important distinction

Note that Feng Shui encompasses a combination of diverse aspects which are woven together. Thus when using colours you must understand the distinction between colour associated with people (that is, with their personal element), colour favouring a certain direction (for example, water colours such as black and blue are for north-facing doors), and colours relating to specific areas in the home independent of the occupants' own personal elements. Do not confuse these categories. They are separate. Although it may coincidentally happen that one colour may satisfy two or more categories, the categories nevertheless remain distinct.

If you are the eldest son, for example, and your personal element is fire, the colours of red, orange and purple would be supportive of your element. These are colours you would wear for an important occasion. Water colours of blue and black would only detract from your fire element. However, in the east part of the home relating to the eldest son, the reverse would hold and water colours would be beneficial. What is relevant in this second case is the specific area of the home and not the individual's personal element.

CHAPTER 9

Buying the Ideal Home

If you are in the fortunate position of searching for a new home for yourself and your family, you can create a blueprint for the best characteristics to look for when you are making your choice.

Of course, we all have to make compromises, but you will be aware of the reasons for those compromises and which features are essential to your choice. You will then know what actions you must take to counteract any remaining negative energies, perhaps with the help of a professional Feng Shui expert.

This chapter will recap the many different aspects which have been discussed throughout the book and which you need to consider when looking at a house. Where the topic has already been covered, you will find solutions or alternatives to the less-than-ideal circumstances in the main chapter. Here, we will also give you some additional information on other important points which have not been dealt with before.

Relating the purchase to your birth year

The best time to move is when your birthdate does not clash with the date you move. This is the Feng Shui expert's domain and is too complex for a book at this level. .

Mountains

Look for a house with a large mountain or building behind it rather than an open space. Any elemental mountain shape apart from the jagged outline of fire is good.

This will impart the strength and support of others.

Rivers

Rivers near the house should be Tong Wan, and this means that the prime aspect for water until the year 2004 is to the east of the house.

Roads

Houses are in the best position on straight or gently curved roads away from sharp bends or junctions. The movement of the traffic along the road is best in little waves and of an unpolluted nature. This will indicate the generation of wealth.

Air

Space in front of the house is a good characteristic. Relate the date of purchase to the Tong Wan chart; the best aspect until 2003 is for the main door to be facing west, although this will depend on how long you intend to remain in the property.

This will maximise your wealth potential and help you enjoy life's comforts.

Yin and Yang

Balance these masculine and feminine elements by looking for a property with an equal number of houses to the left and to the right.

The elements

Choose your elemental colours to complement your own personality and that of the other members of the household.

Shapes of houses

Look for a home which has a shape relating to the element whose characteristics you most need in your home environment. The square and rectangular shapes of earth and wood offer the best security and stability.

Other factors affecting the house

Why is the house for sale?

If the house is being sold because of sudden bankruptcy, this will be bad luck unless the situation was attributable to a general economic depression. Ideally, avoid buying such a house. A Chinese adherent of Feng Shui would not buy a house with significantly negative indicators.

Why is the house vacant?

If the owners have died because of old age, that is obviously a natural occurrence. If, however, the previous occupant died in an accident or before the age of 40, it is best not to move into the house in case you take on their misfortune.

Has there been a fire in the property?

If a fire has occurred more than once, it is a strong indication that it is a fire-prone plot and is best avoided.

Water pipes

Large underground water pipes, other than ordinary domestic pipes, running in a back to front direction and positioned just under the main door symbolise a constant drain of financial resources away from the house. If you cannot remedy this problem, it is better to look for another house.

Tunnels

Properties above underground tunnels are best avoided, as the intermittent vibrations coming from beneath symbolise a general undermining of all your efforts. You should only buy such a house if you can fill in the tunnels.

The ideal house

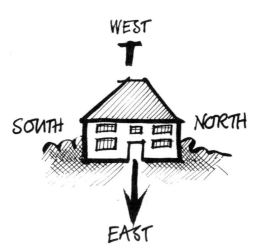

The ideal house has a metal-shaped mountain to the rear, a Dragon on the left and a Tiger on the right. It will have a generous space at the front. A door facing east will bring you good fortune in 1997.

CHAPTER 10

Love, Wealth, Luck and Marriage

To conclude this book, here are some more personal notes on the value of Feng Shui and how it can change your life.

If you imagine that Feng Shui can give you anything you desire, think again. It can only help you to find what you are destined to find by helping you to focus on the positive, to mitigate the negative and to achieve a balance and harmony in your life.

Feng Shui and luck

Feng Shui can, however, have a positive influence on your luck. For instance, you may have been born with a bad lifeline, but through attaining an equilibrium between your living environment and your inner self, you will think positively and generate very positive vibes. If communicated to all you reach, and providing you capitalise on this, luck will be on your side.

Conversely, even if you have a good lifeline but do nothing except lounge around waiting to be showered with unimaginable riches, you could well dream your years away into the next life!

Feng Shui and wealth

To think that Feng Shui will give you riches beyond your dreams is a fallacy. Feng Shui will help you to find what's yours to have, however. That which you are not destined to have, Feng Shui cannot procure for you.

To improve your financial situation

There are various Feng Shui measures you can take to improve your chances of having money and keeping it.

Always keep toilet doors shut.

Screen the entrance from the dining room and rooms beyond from the main door, to prevent your money escaping through the door.

Leave the floor by the main entrance uncluttered.

Feng Shui and love

To increase your chances of meeting someone special, refer to your year of birth in the following table and the section of the house in which you should place a vase. Fill the vase with water, and do not forget to change it every few days. If that special someone should move in to live with you – or you with them – the vase can safely be moved to a new spot.

Vase love chart

Year of birth	Section of house	Year of birth	Section of house
1920	west	1939	north
1921	south	1940	west
1922	east	1941	south
1923	north	1942	east
1924	west	1943	north
1925	south	1944	west
1926	east	1945	south
1927	north	1946	east
1928	west	1947	north
1929	south	1948	west
1930	east	1949	south
1931	north	1950	east
1932	west	1951	north
1933	south	1952	west
1934	east	1953	south
1935	north	1954	east
1936	west	1955	north
1937	south	1956	west
1938	east	1957	south

Year of birth	Section of house	Year of birth	Section of house
1958	east	1980	west
1959	north	1981	south
1960	west	1982	east
1961	south	1983	north
1962	east	1984	west
1963	north	1985	south
1964	west	1986	east
1965	south	1987	north
1966	east	1988	west
1967	north	1989	south
1968	west	1990	east
1969	south	1991	north
1970	east	1992	west
1971	north	1993	south
1972	west	1994	east
1973	south	1995	north
1974	east	1996	west
1975	north	1997	south
1976	west	1998	east
1977	south	1999	north
1978	east	2000	west
1979	north		

Feng Shui and marriage

For marital bliss – on the premise that if you can bury your differences or even call a truce at the end of the day, you are practically there – look up your personal Feng Shui birth year direction (see pages 19–22). Shift your bed into section 1, 2 or 3 as outlined in the relevant pie chart (see pages 23–26).

CHAPTER 11

General Feng Shui for Homes for 1996-1998

As we have seen, Feng Shui has to do with calculating directions in relation to the earth's energy meridian, based upon the interplay of the five elements. As the earth turns upon its axis, so the directions for energy pathways also change with the astral and magnetic influences. Thus, provided you know which direction your main door faces, it is possible to determine which energy will dominate the house in a given year, or even over a 20-year cycle, remembering that the Chinese astrological new year beings on 10 February.

All the following references to the main door refer to the main entrance into your house or flat. Whether it faces the street is irrelevant. The corrective measures suggested will reduce any adverse influences by up to 80 per cent.

We have included a resume of the influences most potent in 1996 so that you can compare the prevalent influences with your own personal experience. You can then look forward and take corrective measures to modify any adverse influences which are likely to be felt in the following year.

Feng Shui for 1996

Main door or bedroom door facing south

1996 was a prosperous year for those with south-facing main or bedroom doors, particularly for those in business and property. Those familiar with Feng Shui would have placed a fish tank with six fish on either side of the main door to enhance this good fortune. Alternatively, a blue or black doormat inside the front door would have brought good luck. A good year in general for financial matters.

Main door or bedroom door facing south-west

Good luck and romance were the main influences in 1996 for those with a south-west facing door. A large vase full of colourful flowers in the south-west section of the sitting room would have encouraged new partnerships for single people. Those trying for a baby boy could have moved their bed to the south-west section of the bedroom and placed a blue carpet or rug underneath it.

Main door or bedroom door facing west

Travel featured strongly in 1996 in the lives of those whose main or bedroom door faced west; it was a good year for those in the travel business. A brown doormat just inside your main door was the most auspicious, and a metal horse in the west side of the sitting room would have brought good luck. Fish tanks in the house in 1996 would have encouraged financial losses.

Main door or bedroom door facing north-west

Roadworks or building works near the main door would have increased the chances of the occupants of these houses being affected by burglary. Red colours and decorative items around the main door would have adversely affected health and financial situation. A white main door would have diluted the negative energies and increased the financial good fortune, which could have been further enhanced by hanging a chimera on either side of the main door, with the mouth of the beast facing towards the door. The bed should have been moved away from the north-west section of the bedroom, and any desks moved out of any room in the north-west section of the home.

Main door or bedroom door facing north

Good news was the main feature of these houses in 1996, with luck enhanced by placing a pink or purple carpet or rug at the front door. Those trying for a baby girl would have increased their chances by moving the bed to the north section of the room and standing it on a red carpet or rug.

Main door or bedroom door facing north-east

A fortunate year, particularly for those in the catering and entertainment industries. Red carpets or decorations near the front door would not have brought good luck. A pair of chimera on either side of the door would have afforded protection, while a round brass clock in the north-east section of the sitting room would have given an even bigger boost to your fortune.

Main door or bedroom door facing east

A good year financially for solicitors and those working in the health profession. Although the health of the occupants of this home may have been adversely affected in 1996, this could have been averted by placing six gold-coloured coins on each side of the east-facing door. A kitchen in the east section of the home could have aggravated skin or digestive problems. Minimal activity in the east section of the house was an advantage, so sofas or televisions in that portion of the house were not well positioned

Main door or bedroom door facing south-east

This door configuration for 1996 indicated bickering and conflict, and the occupants may have found that they were prone to protracted arguments, or discovered that others were gossiping behind their backs. Building or major gardening works near the main doors would have made the occupants more accident prone. A small pink or orange coloured doormat immediately inside the main door and the absence of plants would have been beneficial.

Feng Shui for 1997

Main door or bedroom door facing south

During 1997, this door direction would tend to make occupants prone to gossip or burglary. Activity in the south section of the home in 1997 should be kept to a minimum by moving strategic furniture and clocks away. Chairs should have the backs facing a wall rather than a window, and additional home security might be a consideration. Place a brown or yellow doormat just inside the south-facing door.

Main door or bedroom door facing south-west

1997 offers a triple bonus to the occupants of these houses: a bright outlook in luck, financial prospects and at work in a hectic but rewarding year. Good fortune can be enhanced still further by placing a green rug inside the south-west facing doors.

Main door or bedroom door facing west

There is negative energy at west-facing doors during 1997. To dilute this energy and prevent bad luck financially, paint the main door white and hang a chimera on either side of the main door, with the mouths facing the door. Place a white or cream-coloured doormat immediately inside the main door, and remove all red decorative items from around the door as they could adversely affect your financial situation or your health. If possible, avoid having building or road work near the main door this year. Also, move beds and desks out of the north-west section of the home or in any room that has a west-facing door.

Main door or bedroom door facing north-west

These doors are well positioned to catch the auspicious winds for 1997 which will boost both education and career. Introduce water plants near the main door to focus concentration and stimulate creativity. Place a green doormat just inside the north-west facing doors and move desks into the north-west section of the home.

Main door or bedroom door facing north

These are the most auspicious doors for 1997, and particularly so for people in the catering business. This beneficial energy brings prosperity, good luck and career opportunities. A pink, brown or yellow doormat at the main door will maximise this positive energy.

Main door or bedroom door facing north-east

There are good opportunities for travel in store in 1997 for the occupants of this house, plus it is a good year if you are moving home or offices. Place a black or dark blue doormat at the main door to avoid any potential legal problems. Those in the travel or courier services, including long-distance drivers, could see an increase in their income this year.

Main door or bedroom door facing east

These doors are well positioned to catch the positive energies during 1997 for happiness, love and travel. Place a blue doormat immediately inside the east-facing door to amplify the beneficial energy.

Main door or bedroom door facing south-east

Occupants of homes with south-east facing doors may be prone to health problems in 1997. To correct this imbalance of energies, place six gold-coloured coins on each side of the door. If the kitchen is located in the east side of the home, you may find that you need to be sensitive towards your stomach. Keep activity in the east side of the house to a minimum. Do not place the television or sofa in the east side.

Feng Shui for 1998

Main door or bedroom door facing south

An auspicious year for those in the travel business. You should take care to move any fish tanks away from the south part of the house during 1998 as this could reduce your financial good fortune. For good luck, place six very old gold-coloured coins on each side of the south-facing door.

Main door or bedroom door facing south-west

This year will be smooth going, in particular for business and career-minded people. Remove plants or any green-coloured objects from the area of the door to minimise any negative energies there may be. A red doormat or fish tank with six fish near the main door will enhance all the positive energies which are around in 1998.

Main door or bedroom door facing west

West-facing doors are well placed in 1998 to catch the beneficial winds of the 'four green stars', which can have a positive effect on financial circumstances, particularly for teachers or those working in offices. To capitalise on this, place a dark green doormat at the main door or put plants anywhere in the door area.

Main door or bedroom door facing north-west

1998's configuration for houses with north-west facing doors indicates the possibility of conflict and argument. Minimise the negative energies by placing a red or orange-coloured doormat inside the main door and remove any green plants.

Main door or bedroom door facing north

This is not the most auspicious direction for a main door in 1998, as there are potentially invasive energies denoting the possibility of burglary. Reduce your ill luck by removing decorative items and red colours from the main door area, as these may bring poor financial luck. Place a white doormat just inside the door and a chimera on each side of the door to enhance the positive energies.

Main door or bedroom door facing north-east

Negative energies in these homes may affect both health and finances in 1998. To correct these influences, place six very old gold-coloured coins on each side of the door, or place a chimera on each side of the door, with the faces of the beasts facing towards the door. Painting the door white and placing a white doormat inside the door will also deflect the negative energies.

Main door or bedroom door facing east

In 1998, there will be happy news for those whose main door or bedroom door faces east, and their luck will be good. Place a green rug or doormat just inside the door to enhance the good fortune still further.

Main door or bedroom door facing south-east

In 1998, occupants of houses with south-east facing doors will catch the energy for happiness, love and travel. Place a blue doormat inside the door to maximise your chances of successful love and romance.